New & Updated

GIANT PANDAS

BY GAIL GIBBONS

HOLIDAY HOUSE NEW YORK

Special thanks to Ronald R. Swaisgood, PhD, Brown Chair and Director of Recovery Ecology, San Diego Zoo Global and Chair, Giant Panda Expert Team, International Union for the Conservation of Nature

Thanks also to James Doherty, General Curator Emeritus of the New York Zoological Society, Bronx, New York

To Roger Buttignol

Copyright © 2002, 2021 by Gail Gibbons
All Rights Reserved
HOLIDAY HOUSE is registered in the U.S. Patent and Trademark Office.
Printed and bound in September 2021 at C&C Offset, Shenzhen, China.
www.holidayhouse.com
Second Edition
1 3 5 7 9 10 8 6 4 2

Library of Congress has cataloged the prior edition as follows:
Gibbons, Gail.
Giant pandas / by Gail Gibbons.—1st ed.
p. cm.
Summary: An introduction to the physical characteristics, behavior,
life cycle, and habitat of these endangered animals.
ISBN 978-0-8234-1761-1 (hardcover)
ISBN 978-0-8234-1828-6 (paperback)
1. Giant panda—Juvenile literature. [1. Giant panda.
2. Pandas. 3. Endangered species.] I. Title.
QL737.C214 G55 2002
599.789—dc21 2002019057
ISBN: 978-0-8234-4982-8 (revised hardcover)

GIANT PANDA

Misty, thick clouds hang over the mountaintops. A large black-and-white animal makes its way through a bamboo forest. It is a giant panda.

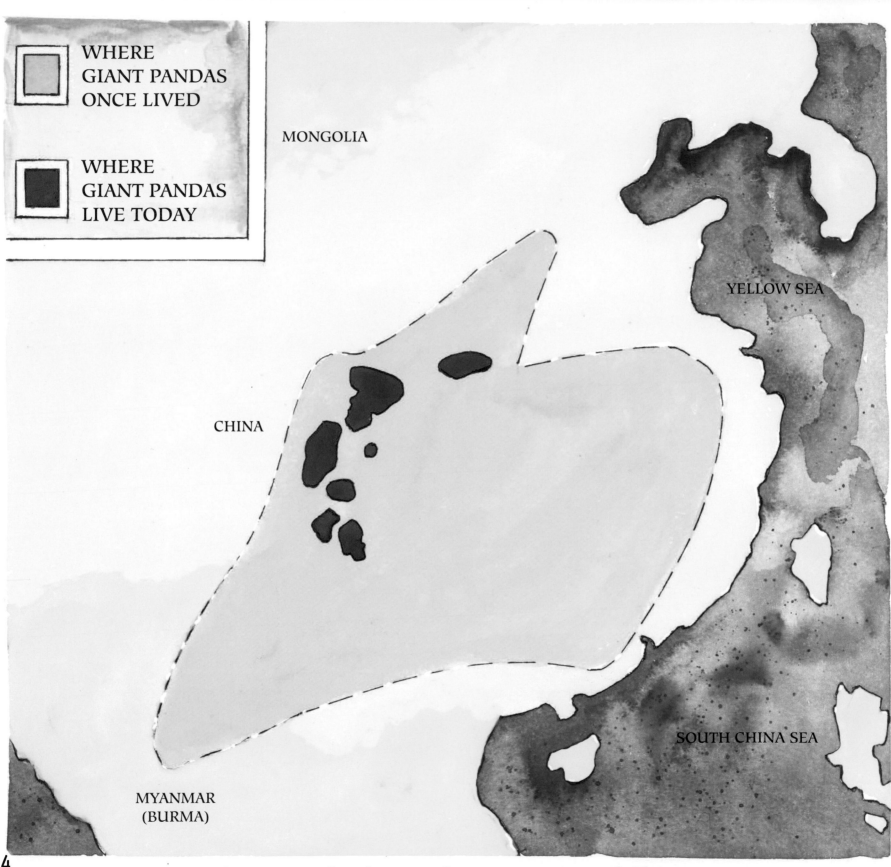

WHERE
GIANT PANDAS
ONCE LIVED

WHERE
GIANT PANDAS
LIVE TODAY

MONGOLIA

YELLOW SEA

CHINA

SOUTH CHINA SEA

MYANMAR
(BURMA)

Giant pandas live in the mountains of China.

The Chinese people call the giant panda da xiong mao
(dah-shiong-mao), meaning "big bear cat." It looks like a
bear and has long claws like a cat.

5

Giant pandas are members of the bear family.

GIANT PANDA CHARACTERISTICS

NECK

EARS

EYE

SNOUT

NOSE

MOUTH

PAWS

CLAWS

Adult giant pandas are about 4 to 5 feet (1.2 to 1.5 m) long and normally weigh about 200 pounds (91 kg). Most of the time they move slowly. But if they want to, they can move at a fast trot. Their bodies are very flexible.

BACK

FUR

Underneath the white
fur is pink skin

TAIL

SCENT GLANDS

STOMACH

Under the black
fur is black skin

LEGS

The fur of a giant panda is thick, coarse, and oily to keep the panda's
body warm and dry. The fur is about 2 inches (5 cm) long.

Giant pandas have poor eyesight, but they have excellent senses of smell and hearing. In fact, pandas are hard to find in the wild because they can hide when they smell or hear people coming.

A bleat means a friendly hello.

Huffing or snorting means "I'm frightened."

Normally giant pandas are shy and tend to stay by themselves. When they want to communicate with one another, they use about eleven different kinds of sounds. They bark, growl, squeal, and make other sounds to mean different things.

Giant pandas also communicate by leaving their scent to tell other pandas they are in the area. They do this by rubbing a smelly liquid from glands under their tails onto rocks or trees.

Thousands of years ago giant pandas ate only meat, but over time their diet changed to mostly plants, mainly bamboo. Occasionally they eat grass, roots, vines, honey, or even meat.

Bamboo! Because bamboo is not very nutritious, giant pandas must spend between ten and sixteen hours a day eating it in order to stay strong and healthy. The average panda eats about 27 pounds (12 kg) of bamboo in a single day.

A "THUMB" is a rigid extension.

CLAWS

Giant pandas have five claws on each of their paws, and they also have a special "thumb" on their front paws. They use their thumbs and claws to grasp the bamboo.

JAWS

TEETH

Giant pandas use their big teeth and powerful jaws to crush
and eat the bamboo stalks. They also eat the leaves.

16

Giant pandas can be playful and athletic. They do somersaults and climb trees quite easily. Also, giant pandas can swim, holding their heads above water while they paddle with their legs.

Giant pandas don't have a regular sleeping place. They sleep on the ground, in the base of a hollow tree, or wherever and whenever they feel tired. They sleep two to four hours at a time.

Male and female giant pandas come together to mate in the spring. After mating, the male goes off on his own. The female makes a bed of bamboo, twigs, and grass in a cave, among rocks, or in a hollow tree. This place is called a den.

Young giant pandas are called CUBS.

A HABITAT is where an animal lives in nature.

In the autumn, about five months later, the mother panda gives birth to one or two babies called cubs. Immediately after giving birth, she begins nursing one of the cubs. A mother will raise only one cub at a time. Only one will survive. In their natural habitat, the mothers usually give birth every one to three years.

A cub is very small. It only weighs about 3 ounces (85 g) and is about 6 inches (15 cm) long. The mother is about nine hundred times larger than her cub. It's amazing how gentle she can be.

The cub has pink skin all over and some fuzzy white fur. Its cry sounds like a human baby. The mother holds her cub almost all the time. She won't leave to get food for herself for about one week after her cub's birth.

In about forty days, the cub opens its eyes. It has black-and-white markings and is still helpless. When the mother wants to move her cub, she gently picks it up by its neck and carries it from place to place.

At about four months old the cub is able to crawl. At seven months old the cub can run and climb trees. It weighs about 20 pounds (9 kg) and is beginning to learn how to eat bamboo.

At about two years old the young giant panda weighs around 120 pounds (54 kg). It has learned all it can from its mother. Now it is time for the young panda to live on its own. In another three years it will be able to have its own young.

The number of giant pandas has become smaller because of the destruction of their natural habitat by people, accidental deaths in traps set for other animals, and disturbance from cattle and other domestic animals invading their habitat.

Over the last several hundred years the number of pandas has decreased a lot. In the 1980s there were only about 1,200 left, but the population has been slowly increasing to more than 1,800 today. The people of China are trying to protect them. They have set aside large areas, called reserves, where giant pandas can live safely. Also, it is a crime to harm or kill a giant panda.

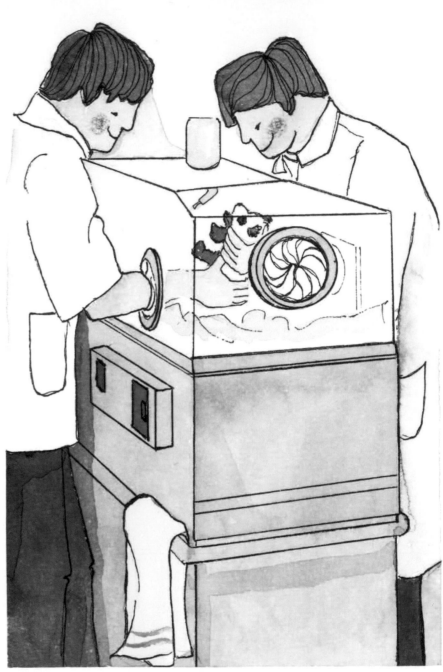

In China and in a small number of other countries, scientists are trying to help increase the population of giant pandas. These pandas are cared for in captivity. The scientists try to encourage the pandas to give birth and care for their cubs.

When the young giant pandas are capable of living on their own, some of them are released back into the wild nature reserves in China. Others are placed in zoos.

Whenever there are giant pandas in a zoo, people love to come see them. They look like big, chubby black-and-white teddy bears that are very playful.

It is so much fun watching them. Giant pandas are one of the rarest and most appealing animals in the world.

PANDAS . . . PANDAS . . . PANDAS . . .

For years, scientists disagreed on what scientific family giant pandas belonged to. Now it is agreed that they are members of the bear family.

The biggest giant panda that was ever weighed was almost 400 pounds (181 kg).

In one year a giant panda may eat about 10,000 pounds (4,536 kg) of bamboo!

A giant panda can live to be twenty-five to thirty years old.

It used to be difficult for scientists to breed and raise pandas, but research has now solved most of these problems. The panda population in captivity has been growing very rapidly, and today there are more than 500 pandas.

China began trying to breed giant pandas in 1955. In September 1963, Ming-Ming became the first cub born in captivity.

There are only a few zoos outside of China that have giant pandas.

All pandas living in zoos are given two names, a Chinese custom that indicates love and affection.

In 1972, China gave two giant pandas, Ling-Ling and Hsing-Hsing (shing-shing), to the National Zoo in Washington, DC.

In 1936, Su-Lin became the first giant panda to be brought to the United States. He was a popular attraction at the Brookfield Zoo in Chicago, Illinois.

Beginning in January 2001, people lined up to see Tian Tian (t-YEN t-YEN) and Mei Xiang (may sh-ONG) at the National Zoo in Washington, DC. They had been flown there from China on a special plane called PandaOne. The pandas have now lived there for more than twenty years.